EASY ITALIAN
SOUPS, PASTA, GNOCCHI & RISOTTO

THICK VEGETABLE SOUP WITH PESTO

MINESTRONE ALLA GENOVESE

SERVES **4**   PREPARATION TIME: **25** MINUTES, PLUS **8** HOURS SOAKING TIME
COOKING TIME: **2** HOURS

150g/5½oz dried **borlotti beans**

3 tbsp **olive oil**

1 large **onion**, sliced

2 sticks **celery**, sliced

1 **carrot**, sliced

2 cloves **garlic**, crushed

100g/3½oz thickly sliced **pancetta**, diced

1 tbsp **tomato purée**

1 litre/1¾ pints/4 cups **chicken** or
   vegetable stock *(see page 36)*

1 x 400g/14oz tin chopped **tomatoes**

2 **potatoes**, peeled and diced

100g/3½oz shelled fresh **peas**

1 **courgette**, diced

100g/3½oz **green beans**, roughly chopped

1 handful **flat-leaf parsley**, roughly chopped

salt and freshly ground **black pepper**

basil pesto *(see page 38)* and freshly grated
   Parmesan cheese, to serve

1 **PLACE** the borlotti beans in a large pan. Cover with cold water and leave to soak for 8 hours or overnight. Drain, rinse several times in cold water and set aside.

2 **HEAT** the olive oil in a large saucepan over a moderate heat. Add the onion, celery and carrot and cook for 3–4 minutes, stirring frequently. Add the garlic and pancetta and cook for another 2 minutes, then stir in the tomato purée until well combined.

3 **STIR** the drained beans into the pan of vegetables, along with the stock and the chopped tomatoes. Lower the heat and leave to simmer for about 1½ hours, until the borlotti beans begin to soften.

4 **ADD** the potatoes, peas, courgette, green beans and parsley and continue to simmer for a further 30 minutes, until the vegetables are tender.

5 **SEASON** to taste with salt and freshly ground pepper and serve in warm bowls, with a spoonful of pesto and a sprinkling of freshly grated Parmesan cheese added just before serving.

VENETIAN PEA AND RICE SOUP

RISI E BISI

SERVES 4   PREPARATION TIME: 20 MINUTES   COOKING TIME: 20 MINUTES

This is a cross between a thick soup and a risotto. You could almost think of it as a "lazy" risotto, as it does not require constant stirring.

---

1 litre/1¾ pints/4 cups **chicken** or **vegetable stock** *(see page 36)*

2 tbsp **olive oil**

60g/2¼oz **butter**

1 small **onion**, diced

55g/2oz thickly sliced **pancetta**, diced

150g/5½oz **risotto rice**

300g/10½oz shelled fresh **peas**

1 small handful fresh **mint**, roughly chopped

4 tbsp freshly grated **Parmesan cheese**

salt and freshly ground **black pepper**

1 **HEAT** the stock in a saucepan until just bubbling. Keep at a gentle simmer. In a large, clean pan heat the olive oil with half the butter. Add the onion and cook over a low heat for about 5 minutes, stirring often, until soft and translucent.

2 **ADD** the pancetta and cook for a further 2 minutes over a medium heat, then add the rice and stir to coat well with the butter mixture.

3 **POUR** in the hot stock, lower the heat and leave to simmer for about 10 minutes, stirring occasionally.

4 **ADD** the peas and cook for a further 5–6 minutes, until they are tender. Remove from the heat, then stir in the remaining butter, the mint and the Parmesan cheese. Season to taste with salt and pepper and serve immediately.

FISH SOUP

ZUPPA DI PESCE

SERVES **4**   PREPARATION TIME: **25** MINUTES   COOKING TIME: **30** MINUTES

This intensely flavoured seafood broth is light and refreshing.

200g/7oz raw **prawns**, shelled

150g/5½oz **monkfish** fillets,
    membrane removed

150g/5½oz **cod**

150g/5½oz shelled **scallops**, roe removed

3 tbsp **olive oil**

1 small stick **celery**, finely diced

1 **carrot**, finely diced

1 bulb **fennel**, finely diced

2 cloves **garlic**, crushed

10 tbsp dry **white wine**

1 x 400g/14oz tin **chopped tomatoes**

1 litre/1¾ pints/4 cups **fish stock** *(see page 37)*

salt and freshly ground **black pepper**

1 handful **flat-leaf parsley**, roughly chopped

1 **PEEL** the prawns and cut the monkfish, cod and scallops into bite-sized pieces. Set aside in the fridge until required.

2 **HEAT** the oil in a large saucepan. Add the celery, carrot and fennel and cook over a medium heat for around 5 minutes, stirring often to prevent browning. Add the garlic and cook another 1 minute.

3 **POUR** in the white wine, chopped tomatoes and fish stock and bring to the boil. Reduce the heat and leave to simmer for 25 minutes.

4 **STIR** in the prepared fish and continue to simmer for a further 5 minutes. Season to taste with salt and pepper and stir in the chopped parsley. Serve immediately.

PASTA AND BEAN SOUP

PASTA E FAGIOLI

SERVES 4 PREPARATION TIME: 20 MINUTES, PLUS 8 HOURS SOAKING TIME
COOKING TIME: 1½ HOURS

This is a typical rustic Italian soup. The swirl of olive oil, added on the top just before serving, helps to enhance the flavour.

300g/10½oz dried **borlotti beans**

2 sprigs fresh **rosemary**

1 tbsp **olive oil**

1 **onion**, diced

2 cloves **garlic**, peeled

1.5 litres/2¾ pints/6 cups **chicken** or **vegetable stock** *(see page 36)*

2 handfuls **flat-leaf parsley**, roughly chopped

salt and freshly ground **black pepper**

100g/3½oz short **pasta tubes**

extra-virgin olive oil, to serve

1 **PLACE** the borlotti beans in a large pan. Cover with cold water and leave to soak for 8 hours or overnight.

2 **DRAIN** the beans and rinse thoroughly. Place in a clean pan and cover with plenty of fresh cold water. Add the rosemary and bring to the boil. Simmer for about 1 hour or until tender. Drain and set on one side.

3 **HEAT** the olive oil in a clean pan, add the onion and cook for about 5 minutes on a very low heat, stirring occasionally. Add the garlic and cook for another minute.

4 **ADD** the drained beans to the pan with the stock and about two-thirds of the parsley and season to taste with salt and pepper. Bring to the boil, lower the heat and leave to simmer for 30 minutes. Allow to cool a little.

5 **TRANSFER** to a blender or food processor and process until smooth (or use an immersion blender). Return to the cleaned pan, add the pasta and cook for 10–12 minutes or until the pasta is tender. Season, if necessary, with salt and pepper.

6 **DIVIDE** between warm serving bowls. Serve topped with a swirl of extra-virgin olive oil and a sprinkling of the remaining parsley.

SPAGHETTI WITH PRAWNS

SPAGHETTI CON GAMBERETTI

SERVES 4 PREPARATION TIME: 10 MINUTES COOKING TIME: 12 MINUTES

This simple yet elegant pasta dish is quick to prepare and packed with flavour.

400g/14oz dried **spaghetti**

2 tbsp **extra-virgin olive oil**

25g/1oz **butter**

1 small **onion**, finely diced

300g/10½oz raw **prawns**, shelled

3 **tomatoes**, diced

7 tbsp dry **white wine**

salt and freshly ground **black pepper**

1 small handful fresh **basil leaves**, torn

1 BRING a large pan of salted water to the boil. Add the spaghetti and cook, according to the packet instructions, until tender. Drain.

2 HEAT the olive oil and butter in another large saucepan while the pasta is cooking. Add the onion and cook, stirring frequently, for about 5 minutes, until soft.

3 ADD the prawns to the softened onion and continue cooking until they start to turn pink. Stir in the tomatoes and white wine, then season to taste with salt and pepper.

4 TOSS the prawn mixture and the basil with the freshly cooked pasta, until well mixed. Adjust the seasoning if needed and serve immediately.

SPAGHETTI WITH BREADCRUMBS

SPAGHETTI CON LA MOLLICA

SERVES **4**   PREPARATION TIME: **10** MINUTES   COOKING TIME: **12** MINUTES

The crunch of the breadcrumbs lends a surprising touch to this dish and adds a truly satisfying dimension to every mouthful.

---

5 tbsp **olive oil**

100g/3½oz **anchovies**, rinsed and drained

2 cloves **garlic**, crushed

100g/3½oz fresh **white breadcrumbs**

400g/14oz dried **spaghetti**

5 tbsp stoned **black olives**, sliced

1 tbsp **capers**, rinsed

juice and grated rind of 1 **lemon**

freshly ground **black pepper**

1 **HEAT** 2 tablespoons of olive oil in a small saucepan. Add the anchovies and cook until they form a paste. Add the garlic and cook for another minute. Set on one side.

2 **HEAT** the remaining oil in a large frying pan. Add the breadcrumbs and stir well to combine with the oil, then continue to cook until the breadcrumbs become golden brown. Remove from the heat and set aside.

3 **COOK** the spaghetti, according to the packet instructions, until tender, and drain.

4 **MIX** the freshly cooked pasta, the anchovy paste, breadcrumbs, olives, capers and lemon juice and rind. Season to taste with black pepper and serve immediately.

THREE CHEESE RAVIOLI WITH BUTTER AND BASIL *RAVIOLI AI TRE FORMAGGI CON BURRO E BASILICO*

SERVES 4   PREPARATION TIME: 40 MINUTES   COOKING TIME: 10 MINUTES

The delicate flavour of these light pasta parcels is enhanced by the addition of extra-virgin olive oil, fragrant fresh basil and a dash of mouth-tingling lemon.

250g/9oz **ricotta cheese**

75g/2½oz freshly grated **pecorino cheese**

70g/2½oz freshly grated **Parmesan cheese**, plus extra for serving

1 small handful fresh **basil leaves**, shredded, plus extra for serving

salt and freshly ground **black pepper**

1 recipe quantity **fresh pasta** dough *(see page 39)*

1 tbsp **olive oil**

3 tbsp **extra-virgin olive oil**

25g/1oz **butter**, melted

juice and grated rind of 1 **lemon**

1 **MIX** the ricotta, pecorino and Parmesan cheeses with the basil in a bowl. Season with a little salt and plenty of pepper and set aside.

2 **CUT** the pasta dough into 4 pieces and roll out each one up to the second thinnest setting on the pasta machine. Lay 1 sheet of pasta on a well-floured surface and place 12 heaped teaspoons of the cheese mixture at equal intervals along it, allowing enough space around each to seal the ravioli. Brush around each heap of cheese mixture with a little water.

3 **PLACE** a second pasta sheet on top. Press down gently around the heaps of cheese filling to seal the 2 sheets of pasta together, making sure no excess air is trapped around the filling. With a sharp knife, cut into 12 individual ravioli. Repeat this process with the remaining 2 sheets of pasta to prepare 12 more ravioli.

4 **BOIL** a large saucepan of salted water. Add the tablespoon of olive oil, then the ravioli, and cook for about 5 minutes, until the pasta is tender but still has some bite. Carefully lift out of the water and drain using a slotted spoon. Divide between 4 warm serving plates.

5 **MIX** together the extra-virgin olive oil, melted butter and lemon juice and rind in a bowl and season to taste with pepper. Drizzle over the ravioli and serve with a sprinkling of shredded basil and grated Parmesan.

BAKED LASAGNE

LASAGNE AL FORNO

SERVES 4–6   PREPARATION TIME: 35 MINUTES, PLUS 2–3 HOURS COOKING TIME FOR SAUCE   COOKING TIME: 40–45 MINUTES

Nothing beats the flavour of a traditional, homemade lasagne. The layers should be distinct and oozing with rich warming ragù sauce and creamy béchamel.

4 tbsp **olive oil**

1 **onion**, diced

1 **carrot**, finely diced

2 sticks **celery**, finely diced

100g/3½oz thickly sliced **pancetta**, diced

500g/1lb 2oz lean minced **beef**

500g/1lb 2oz minced **veal**

250ml/9fl oz/1 cup **milk**

250ml/9fl oz/1 cup **white wine**

1 x 400g/14oz tin chopped **tomatoes**

1 x 500g/1lb 2oz jar **passata**

500ml/17fl oz/2 cups **water**

salt and freshly ground **black pepper**

1 recipe quantity **fresh pasta** sheets *(see page 39)*

1 recipe quantity **béchamel sauce** *(see page 38)*

4 tbsp freshly grated **Parmesan cheese**

1 **HEAT** the olive oil in a large pan over a low heat. Add the onion and cook for 2–3 minutes, until soft. Add the carrot and celery, and cook for another 2 minutes.

2 **TURN** up the heat, add the pancetta and cook, stirring, for 1 minute. Add the beef and veal and cook until the meat has browned. Pour in the milk and allow to boil vigorously until all the liquid has evaporated.

3 **ADD** the wine, tomatoes and passata and turn the heat down to very low. Pour in the water and season to taste with salt and pepper. Simmer very gently for about 2–3 hours to let the flavours fully develop, adding extra water if required to prevent the sauce becoming too dry. Set on one side to cool until needed. Preheat the oven to 180°C/350°F/Gas 4.

4 **CUT** the fresh pasta sheets into pieces that will fit the base of an ovenproof dish, approximately 26cm/10½in by 20cm/8in. Layer the pasta with the meat sauce and béchamel sauce into the dish, starting with a layer of pasta and ending with a layer of béchamel. Sprinkle the Parmesan cheese over the top.

5 **BAKE** in the hot oven for 40–45 minutes, until lightly browned and bubbling. Serve.

"ANGRY" PASTA

PENNE ALL'ARRABBIATA

SERVES **4**   PREPARATION TIME: **15** MINUTES   COOKING TIME: **20** MINUTES

This dish is typically served very hot and spicy, hence its name. But you can make it as mild or as fiery as you prefer, by increasing or decreasing the number of chillies you use when preparing the sauce.

2 tbsp **olive oil**

1 **onion**, sliced

2 **red chillies**, deseeded and finely diced

200g/7oz thickly sliced **pancetta**, diced

1 clove **garlic**, crushed

2 x 400g/14oz tins chopped **tomatoes**

7 tbsp dry **white wine**

400g/14oz dried **penne pasta**

1 handful **flat-leaf parsley**, chopped roughly

freshly shaved or grated **Parmesan cheese**, to serve

1 **HEAT** the oil in a large sauté pan. Add the onion and cook over a moderate heat for 3 minutes, stirring often to prevent browning. Add the chilli, pancetta and garlic and continue cooking for another 2 minutes.

2 **STIR** in the tomatoes and white wine. Lower the heat and leave to simmer for 15 minutes, until the sauce has thickened. Set on one side and keep warm.

3 **COOK** the penne in plenty of boiling salted water, according to the packet instructions, until it is tender but still retains some bite. Drain and toss with the warm sauce and the chopped parsley. Serve with the Parmesan cheese.

SPAGHETTI CARBONARA

SPAGHETTI ALLA CARBONARA

SERVES 4   PREPARATION TIME: 10 MINUTES   COOKING TIME: 12 MINUTES

This perennially popular recipe originated in the Lazio region of Italy, which has Rome at its centre, but it can now be found all over Italy.

---

2 **eggs**

2 tbsp freshly grated **Parmesan cheese**, plus extra to serve

2 tbsp freshly grated **pecorino cheese**

1 tbsp **olive oil**

25g/1oz **butter**

1 clove **garlic**, crushed

175g/6oz thickly sliced **pancetta**, diced

400g/14oz dried **spaghetti**

salt and freshly ground **black pepper**

1 **WHISK** together the eggs, Parmesan and pecorino in a bowl and set on one side.

2 **HEAT** the olive oil and butter in a frying pan. Add the garlic and pancetta and cook over a medium heat until the pancetta is crisp and the garlic is golden brown. Discard the garlic and set the pancetta aside.

3 **COOK** the spaghetti in plenty of salted boiling water, according to the instructions on the packet, until tender but still retaining some bite.

4 **DRAIN** the pasta, then return it to the pan. Toss in the egg mixture and the cooked pancetta and combine well. Season to taste with salt and pepper and serve immediately, with extra grated Parmesan sprinkled over the top if desired.

SPINACH AND RICOTTA RAVIOLI

RAVIOLI DI RICOTTA E SPINACI

SERVES 4   PREPARATION TIME: 40 MINUTES   COOKING TIME: 10 MINUTES

With their subtle flavourings of ricotta cheese, spinach and nutmeg, these traditional ravioli are mouth-wateringly delicious.

400g/14oz fresh **spinach**, rinsed thoroughly

25g/1oz **butter**

1 small **onion**, diced

2 tbsp grated **Parmesan cheese**,
   plus extra for serving

250g/9oz **ricotta cheese**

½ tsp freshly grated **nutmeg**

salt and freshly ground **black pepper**

1 recipe quantity **fresh pasta** dough *(see page 39)*

85g/3oz **butter**, melted

1 **COOK** the spinach in a small amount of boiling water until just wilted. Drain, squeeze out as much water as possible, chop finely and set aside.

2 **MELT** the butter in a pan over a low heat. Add the onion and cook for 3–4 minutes until soft. Off the heat, stir in the spinach, Parmesan, ricotta and nutmeg. Season to taste with salt and pepper and set aside.

3 **CUT** the pasta dough into 4 pieces and roll out each one up to the second thinnest setting on the pasta machine. Lay 1 pasta sheet on a floured surface and place 12 heaped teaspoons of the spinach mixture at equal intervals along it, allowing enough space around each to seal the ravioli. Brush around each heap of spinach mixture with a little water.

4 **PLACE** a second pasta sheet on top. Press down gently around the heaps of filling to seal the 2 sheets of pasta together, ensuring no excess air is trapped around the filling. With a sharp knife, cut into 12 individual ravioli. Repeat with the remaining pasta sheets and filling.

5 **BOIL** a large saucepan of salted water. Add the ravioli and cook for 5 minutes, or until the pasta is just tender. Lift out of the pan and drain, using a slotted spoon, then divide between 4 warm serving plates.

6 **DRIZZLE** the melted butter over the top of the ravioli, sprinkle with some freshly grated Parmesan cheese and serve.

POTATO GNOCCHI WITH BASIL, MOZZARELLA AND ROASTED CHERRY TOMATOES *GNOCCHI DI PATATE*

SERVES 4   PREPARATION TIME: 40 MINUTES   COOKING TIME: 5 MINUTES

Using a potato ricer will produce the lightest possible gnocchi. If you do not have one, however, you can simply mash them.

200g/7oz **cherry tomatoes**

1 tbsp **olive oil**

1kg/2lb 4oz **potatoes**, wrapped in foil and baked in the oven until very soft

200g/7oz **plain flour**

1 **egg**, lightly beaten

salt and freshly ground **black pepper**

3 tbsp **basil pesto** *(see page 38)*

1 small handful baby **mozzarella cheeses**, halved

freshly grated **Parmesan cheese**, to serve

1 **PREHEAT** the oven to 200°C/400°F/Gas 6. Arrange the cherry tomatoes on a baking tray, sprinkle over the olive oil and cook in the hot oven until just soft. Set on one side.

2 **SCOOP** the flesh out of the potatoes, discarding the skins, and press through a potato ricer (or simply mash). Place in a large bowl with the flour and egg and stir to combine. Season to taste with salt and pepper, then tip onto a floured surface and knead to form a soft, pliable dough.

3 **SHAPE** the dough into long cylinders approximately 1.5cm/⅔in in diameter, then cut each one into 2cm/¾in lengths. Mark these gnocchi lengths lightly with the back of a fork, then arrange on a tray that has been lightly dusted with flour.

4 **BRING** a large pan of salted water to the boil. Add the gnocchi and cook for about 5 minutes, or until the gnocchi rise to the top of the water. Lift out of the pan and drain, using a slotted spoon.

5 **PLACE** the hot gnocchi in a large bowl with the pesto, mozzarella and cherry tomatoes and toss gently to combine. Serve immediately, sprinkled with freshly grated Parmesan cheese.

SEMOLINA GNOCCHI WITH FRESH TOMATO SAUCE

GNOCCHI ALLA ROMANA

**SERVES 4–6 PREPARATION TIME: 20 MINUTES, PLUS 1 HOUR COOLING TIME
COOKING TIME: 20 MINUTES**

This is real comfort food. Just serve with a simple green salad.

1 litre/1¾ pints/4 cups **milk**

salt and freshly ground **black pepper**

250g/9oz **semolina**

2 **egg yolks**

200g/7oz **Parmesan cheese**, freshly grated

100g/3½oz **butter**, chopped

1 recipe quantity **fresh tomato sauce**
 (see page 37)

1 **HEAT** the milk in a saucepan with a little salt and pepper until it is just starting to boil.

2 **WHISK** in the semolina, then cook for about 10 minutes over a low heat, stirring constantly with a wooden spoon, until the mixture becomes quite thick.

3 **REMOVE** from the heat and add the egg yolks, half the Parmesan cheese and half the butter.

4 **SPREAD** the mixture over a large baking tray, lined with greaseproof paper, to a depth of about 1cm/½in. Leave to cool for 1 hour.

5 **PREHEAT** the oven to 200°C/400°F/Gas 6. Grease an ovenproof dish with a little of the remaining butter.

6 **CUT** circles out from the cooled gnocchi mixture, using a biscuit cutter, and arrange in a single layer in the greased dish. Dot with the remaining butter. Spoon over the tomato sauce and sprinkle over the remaining Parmesan cheese.

7 **BAKE** the gnocchi in the hot oven for about 20 minutes, until golden brown and bubbling. Serve immediately.

SAFFRON RISOTTO

RISOTTO ALLA MILANESE

SERVES 4   PREPARATION TIME: 10 MINUTES   COOKING TIME: 20 MINUTES

The saffron gives this risotto a rich yellow colour and intense flavour.

---

1 litre/1¾ pints/4 cups **chicken** or **vegetable stock** *(see page 36)*

85g/3oz **butter**

1 small **onion**, diced

300g/10½oz **risotto rice**

125ml/4fl oz/½ cup **white wine**

¼ tsp **saffron threads**, soaked in 2 tbsp boiling water for 10 minutes, water reserved

4 tbsp freshly grated **Parmesan cheese**, plus extra for serving

salt and freshly ground **black pepper**

1 **HEAT** the stock over a medium heat until just beginning to boil. Lower the heat and leave to simmer very gently.

2 **MELT** 60g/2oz of the butter in another saucepan. Add the onion and cook over a low heat for around 5 minutes, until soft but not brown.

3 **ADD** the rice and toast for 2 minutes, stirring constantly, then add the white wine and stir until it has evaporated. Add a ladleful of the hot stock and cook, stirring constantly, until it has all been absorbed by the rice. Continue in this way, adding the saffron and its soaking liquid after the first 10 minutes of cooking, until the rice is just tender but still retains some bite and is creamy in consistency. (It may not be necessary to use all the stock.)

4 **STIR** in the remaining butter and the Parmesan cheese and season to taste with salt and pepper. Leave to stand, covered, for 1–2 minutes, then serve with extra freshly grated Parmesan cheese.

ASPARAGUS RISOTTO

RISOTTO CON ASPARAGI

SERVES 4   PREPARATION TIME: 10 MINUTES   COOKING TIME: 20 MINUTES

The freshness of the asparagus combines superbly with the creaminess of the risotto rice in this truly sublime dish.

500g/1lb 2oz **green asparagus**, trimmed

1 litre/1¾ pints/4 cups **chicken** or **vegetable stock** *(see page 36)*

85g/3oz **butter**

1 small **onion**, finely diced

300g/10½oz **risotto rice**

4 tbsp freshly grated **Parmesan cheese**, plus extra for serving (optional)

salt and freshly ground **black pepper**

1 **COOK** the asparagus in a pan of boiling salted water until just starting to soften. Drain, rinse under cold running water to cool, then pat dry on kitchen paper. Cut into bite-sized chunks and set on one side.

2 **HEAT** the stock over a medium heat until just beginning to boil. Lower the heat and leave to simmer very gently.

3 **MELT** 60g/2¼oz of the butter in another saucepan. Add the onion and cook over a low heat for 3–4 minutes, until soft but not brown.

4 **STIR** in the rice and allow to toast for 2 minutes, then add a ladleful of the hot stock and cook, stirring constantly, until it has all been absorbed by the rice. Continue in this way, adding hot stock and stirring, until the rice is just tender but still retains some bite and is creamy in consistency. (It may not be necessary to use all the stock.)

5 **STIR** in the asparagus, the remaining butter and the Parmesan cheese and adjust the seasoning if necessary. Leave to stand, covered, for 1–2 minutes, then serve with extra freshly grated Parmesan cheese sprinkled over the top, if desired.

MUSHROOM RISOTTO

RISOTTO AI FUNGHI

SERVES 4   PREPARATION TIME: 10 MINUTES   COOKING TIME: 20 MINUTES

Risotto makes a great meal at any time and one of the best ways of flavouring it is by cooking it with wild mushrooms.

400g/14oz mixed **wild mushrooms**

150g/5½oz **butter**

1 litre/1¾ pints/4 cups **chicken** or **vegetable stock** *(see page 36)*

1 small **onion**, diced

300g/10½oz **risotto rice**

4 tbsp freshly grated **Parmesan cheese**, plus extra for serving (optional)

salt and freshly ground **black pepper**

1 WIPE the mushrooms thoroughly and slice thinly. Heat 50g/1¾oz of the butter in a sauté pan and cook the mushrooms for about 4–5 minutes, until soft. Remove from the pan and set aside.

2 HEAT the stock over a medium heat until just beginning to boil. Lower the heat and leave to simmer very gently.

3 MELT 60g/2¼oz of the butter in another saucepan. Add the onion and cook over a low heat for 3–4 minutes, until soft but not brown.

4 STIR in the rice and allow to toast for 2 minutes, then add a ladleful of the hot stock and cook, stirring constantly, until it has all been absorbed by the rice. Continue in this way, adding hot stock and stirring, until the rice is just tender but still retains some bite and is creamy in consistency. (It may not be necessary to use all the stock.)

5 STIR in the mushrooms, the remaining butter and Parmesan cheese and adjust the seasoning if necessary. Leave to stand, covered, for 1–2 minutes, then serve with extra freshly grated Parmesan cheese sprinkled over the top, if desired.

RISOTTO WITH PRAWNS AND CHAMPAGNE

RISOTTO ALLO CHAMPAGNE CON GAMBERETTI

SERVES **4**   PREPARATION TIME: **15** MINUTES   COOKING TIME: **20** MINUTES

Make this for a special celebration meal, or anytime you feel indulgent.

200g/7oz raw **prawns**, shelled

750ml/1½ pints/3 cups **fish stock** *(see page 37)*

85g/3oz **butter**

1 small **onion**, finely diced

1 clove **garlic**, crushed

300g/10½oz **risotto rice**

200ml/7fl oz/¾ cup **Champagne**

salt and freshly ground **black pepper**

1 **RINSE** the prawns, cut in half horizontally and keep refrigerated until required.

2 **HEAT** the stock over a medium heat until just beginning to boil. Lower the heat and leave to simmer very gently.

3 **MELT** 60g/2¼oz of the butter in another saucepan. Add the onion and garlic and cook over a low heat for 3–4 minutes, until soft but not brown.

4 **ADD** the rice and toast for 1 minute, stirring constantly, then pour over half of the Champagne and keep stirring until it has evaporated.

5 **POUR** in a ladleful of the hot stock and cook, stirring constantly, until it has all been absorbed by the rice. Continue in this way, adding hot stock and stirring, until the rice is just tender but still retains some bite and has a creamy consistency. (It may not be necessary to use all the stock.)

6 **TOSS** in the prawns and cook a further minute until they turn pink. Stir in the remaining Champagne and butter and season to taste with salt and pepper. Serve immediately.

STOCKS AND SAUCES

CHICKEN STOCK
BRODO DI POLLO

MAKES 2 LITRES/3½ PINTS/8 CUPS
PREPARATION TIME: 15 MINUTES   COOKING TIME: 2½ HOURS

If you have trouble finding chicken carcasses, substitute with chicken wings. They will render more fat, but this can easily be removed from the surface of the stock after it has been chilled overnight in the fridge.

1kg/2lb 4oz fresh **chicken** carcasses, chopped

1 **onion** (skin left on), cut into quarters

1 **carrot**, roughly chopped

1 bulb **garlic**, cut in half horizontally

1 stick **celery**, roughly chopped

4 **black peppercorns**

1 small handful **flat-leaf parsley**, roughly chopped

2 **bay leaves**

6 litres/10½ pints/24 cups cold **water**

1 **PLACE** all of the ingredients in a large saucepan and bring gently to the boil.

2 **SKIM** off any foam and sediment from the surface, then lower the heat and leave to simmer for around 2½ hours.

3 **STRAIN** the stock through a fine sieve into a clean bowl. Cover and leave to cool completely.

4 **REFRIGERATE** overnight, then skim off any fat from the surface and use as required. It will keep for 3–4 days in the fridge and up to 3 months in the freezer.

VEGETABLE STOCK
BRODO DI VERDURA

MAKES 1.2 LITRES/2 PINTS/4¾ CUPS
PREPARATION TIME: 15 MINUTES   COOKING TIME: 1 HOUR

1 stick **celery**, roughly chopped, plus any leaves from the top of the stalk

1 **carrot**, roughly chopped

1 **onion**, skin removed and sliced

1 bulb **garlic**, cut in half horizontally

2 **bay leaves**

6 **black peppercorns**

1 small handful **flat-leaf parsley**, roughly chopped

1.75 litres/3 pints/7 cups cold **water**

1 **PLACE** all of the ingredients in a large saucepan and bring to the boil over a medium heat.

2 **LOWER** the heat and leave to simmer gently for 1 hour. Remove from the heat and leave to cool.

3 **STRAIN** the stock, pushing down on the vegetables gently to extract the maximum amount of flavour. Use as required. It will keep for up to 4 days in the fridge and for up to 3 months in the freezer.

FISH STOCK
BRODO DI PESCE

MAKES **2** LITRES/**3**½ PINTS/**8** CUPS
PREPARATION TIME: **10** MINUTES   COOKING TIME: **20** MINUTES

15g/½oz **butter**

1 **onion**, roughly chopped

1kg/2lb 4oz **fish** bones, washed and chopped

125ml/4fl oz/½ cup **dry white wine**

2.5 litres/4½ pints/10 cups cold **water**

1 **bay leaf**

4 **black peppercorns**

1 small handful **flat-leaf parsley**, roughly chopped

1 small stick **celery**, roughly chopped

1 **MELT** the butter in a large saucepan over a low heat. Add the onion and cook for 2–3 minutes, until soft but not brown. Add the fish bones and cook for about 1 minute, then pour over the white wine, turn up the heat, and boil until all the wine has evaporated.

2 **ADD** the water, bay leaf, peppercorns, parsley and celery and bring to the boil. Skim off any froth and sediment from the surface, then turn down the heat and leave to simmer gently for 20 minutes, skimming often.

3 **STRAIN** and leave to cool. Use as needed. It will keep for 3–4 days in the fridge and up to 3 months in the freezer.

FRESH TOMATO SAUCE
SALSA FRESCA DI POMODORO

MAKES **500**ML/**17**FL OZ/**2** CUPS
PREPARATION TIME: **15** MINUTES   COOKING TIME: **30** MINUTES

Try to use ripe, in-season tomatoes for this recipe. Tinned tomatoes, however, can be substituted when good fresh ones are unavailable.

2 tbsp **olive oil**

1 **onion**, diced

1 clove **garlic**, crushed

1kg/2lb 4oz fresh **plum tomatoes**, peeled, deseeded and chopped

6 fresh **basil leaves**

1 tsp **balsamic vinegar**

1 tsp **sugar**

salt and freshly ground **black pepper**

1 **HEAT** the oil in a wide-based pan. Add the onion and cook for 3–4 minutes until it is soft and transparent. Add the garlic and cook for another minute.

2 **STIR** in the tomatoes, basil, balsamic vinegar and sugar and leave to simmer for 30 minutes, stirring occasionally.

3 **SEASON** to taste with salt and pepper, then tip into a blender or food processor and process until smooth. Use as required. It can be stored in the fridge for 2–3 days, but is best stored frozen – use within 3 months.

BÉCHAMEL SAUCE

MAKES 1 LITRE/1¾ PINTS/4 CUPS
PREPARATION TIME: 10 MINUTES   COOKING TIME: 10 MINUTES

This simple white sauce makes its appearance in the lasagne recipe on page 85, but is also added to all kinds of other dishes.

1 litre/1¾ pints/4 cups **milk**

½ small **onion**

1 **bay leaf**

1 whole **clove**

85g/3oz **butter**

85g/3oz **plain flour**

salt and freshly ground **black pepper**

grating of fresh **nutmeg**

1 **PLACE** the milk, onion, bay leaf and clove in a medium saucepan and heat gently. As soon as the milk starts to simmer, remove from the heat and leave on one side for at least 10 minutes. Strain, discarding the solids, and set aside.

2 **MELT** the butter in a clean saucepan. Stir in the flour, then allow to cook over a low heat for 2–3 minutes, taking care not to let the mixture brown. Remove from the heat.

3 **WHISK** the milk into the butter and flour mixture, then return to a low heat and continue to whisk until the sauce is smooth and thick. Leave to simmer very gently for about 3 minutes. Season to taste with salt, pepper and nutmeg and use as required.

BASIL PESTO
PESTO

MAKES 250ML/9FL OZ/1 CUP
PREPARATION TIME: 15 MINUTES

This simple sauce is absolutely bursting with flavour. It can be made in advance and kept in the fridge, ready to simply stir into a plate of freshly cooked pasta to create a quick and delicious meal. To store, place in an airtight container, top with a splash of extra-virgin olive oil and refrigerate. It will keep for approximately 2 weeks.

3 large handfuls fresh **basil leaves**

25g/1oz **pine nuts**

2 large cloves **garlic**, chopped

1 tbsp **sea salt**

freshly ground **black pepper**

10 tbsp **extra-virgin olive oil**

50g/2oz **Parmesan cheese**, grated

1 **PLACE** the basil, pine nuts, garlic, and salt and pepper to taste in a large bowl.

2 **ADD** the olive oil and blend, using a hand-held mixer or blender, to form a paste. Alternatively, process the ingredients in a blender or food processor.

3 **STIR** in the Parmesan cheese, taste and readjust the seasoning if necessary. Use as required.

PASTA

FRESH PASTA

SERVES 4 AS A MAIN COURSE; 8 AS A STARTER
PREPARATION TIME: 30 MINUTES
COOKING TIME: 4 MINUTES, PLUS 30 MINUTES RESTING TIME

The silky texture of freshly made pasta is well worth the effort that goes into preparing it yourself at home. For the best result, use specialized 00 flour – often labelled as "pasta flour" – which is now readily available from many supermarkets as well as speciality stores. A food processor makes mixing the dough easier, but it can also be mixed by hand. To roll out the pasta, you ideally need a good quality, manual pasta machine.

250g/9oz 00 (pasta) **flour**

6 large **egg yolks**

1 **egg**

1½ tbsp **olive oil**

1 tbsp **milk**

1 **PLACE** the flour in the bowl of a food processor. Whisk together the egg yolks, whole egg, olive oil and milk in a jug.

2 **WITH** the motor running, slowly pour the liquid mixture through the feeding tube onto the flour in the processor, until a soft ball of dough is just starting to form. Take care not to add too much liquid – depending on the weather, the dough may need more or less to come together. Wrap in clear film, set aside and allow to rest for 30 minutes.

3 **DIVIDE** the dough in two and set one half aside in a cool place, wrapped in clear film to prevent it from drying out.

4 **SET** the pasta machine to its widest setting and use to roll out the unwrapped half of dough. Fold the rolled dough in half and roll it once more through the machine. Repeat this process 10 more times, folding the dough in half each time before passing it through the machine.

5 **CONTINUE** rolling the dough in this way, but without folding it in half, and lower the setting on the machine by one notch each time, until it has passed through on the second narrowest setting (any narrower and it tends to fall apart).

6 **LAY** the sheet of dough on a lightly floured board. Cut into the desired shapes with a sharp knife or cutter and leave to dry.

7 **REPEAT** with the remaining half of the dough.

8 **BRING** a large pot of salted water to the boil. Add the pasta and stir well to prevent it sticking. Return to the boil, lower the heat and leave to simmer for about 4 minutes, or until the pasta has floated to the top and is paler in colour. Drain and serve immediately with your chosen sauce.

VARIATIONS

PASTA WITH FRESH HERBS – Add 3 tablespoons of finely chopped, fresh, mixed herbs – such as oregano, flat-leaf parsley and thyme – to the flour. Proceed as for basic recipe.

TOMATO PASTA – Beat 2 tablespoons of tomato purée into the egg mixture. Proceed as for the basic recipe.

SPINACH PASTA – Use only 3 egg yolks. Add 150g/5½oz cooked spinach, that has been squeezed until very dry, to flour in the food processor and pulse briefly to combine. Proceed as for the basic recipe.

Easy Italian Soups, Pasta, Gnocchi & Risotto

Jennifer Donovan

This edition first published in the United Kingdom and Ireland in 2012 by
Siena Books, an imprint of Duncan Baird Publishers Ltd
Sixth Floor, Castle House
75–76 Wells Street
London W1T 3QH

Conceived, created and designed by Duncan Baird Publishers

Managing Editor: Grace Cheetham
Editor: Cécile Landau
Designer: Luana Gobbo
Studio Photography: William Lingwood
Photography Assistant: Alice Deuchar
Stylists: Bridget Sargeson and Stella Sargeson (food)
    and Helen Trent (props)

British Library Cataloguing-in-Publication Data:
A CIP record for this book is available from the British Library

ISBN: 978-1-84899-098-2

10 9 8 7 6 5 4 3 2 1

Typeset in Spectrum and Univers
Colour reproduction by Scanhouse, Malaysia
Printed in China by Imago

Publisher's note

While every care has been taken in compiling the recipes for this book,
Duncan Baird Publishers, or any other persons who have been involved
in working on this publication, cannot accept responsibility for any errors
or omissions, inadvertent or not, that may be found in the recipes or text,
nor for any problems that may arise as a result of preparing one of these
recipes. If you are pregnant or breastfeeding or have any special dietary
requirements or medical conditions, it is advisable to consult a medical
professional before following any of the recipes contained in this book.

Notes on the recipes

Unless otherwise stated:
- Use medium eggs
- Use fresh herbs
- Do not mix metric and imperial measurements
- 1 tsp = 5ml
  1 tbsp = 15ml
  1 cup = 250ml